MAR 0 7 2008

What's So Great About...? DAVY CROCKETT

Russell Roberts

P.O. Box 196
Hockessin, Delaware 19707
Visit us on the web: www.mitchelllane.com
Comments? email us: mitchelllane@mitchelllane.com

Printing   1   2   3   4   5   6   7   8   9

A Robbie Reader/What's So Great About . . . ?

Annie Oakley	Daniel Boone	**Davy Crockett**
Ferdinand Magellan	Francis Scott Key	Henry Hudson
Jacques Cartier	Johnny Appleseed	Robert Fulton
Sam Houston		

Library of Congress Cataloging-in-Publication Data
Roberts, Russell.
    Davy Crockett / by Russell Roberts.
      p. cm. — (A Robbie Reader. What's So Great About . . . ?)
    Includes bibliographical references and index.
    ISBN 1-58415-476-4 (library bound: alk. paper)
    1. Crockett, Davy, 1786–1836—Juvenile literature. 2. United States. Congress. House—Biography—Juvenile literature. 3. Pioneers—Tennessee—Biography—Juvenile literature. 4. Frontier and pioneer life—Tennessee—Juvenile literature. 5. Legislators—United States—Biography—Juvenile literature. 6. Tennessee—Biography—Juvenile literature. 7. Alamo (San Antonio, Tex.)—Seige, 1836—Juvenile literature. I. Title. II. Series.
F436.C95R63 2006
978.8'04092–dc22
                                                                    2005028494
ISBN-10: 1-58415-476-4   ISBN-13: 978-1-58415-476-1

ABOUT THE AUTHOR: Russell Roberts has written and published nearly 40 books for adults and children on a variety of subjects, including baseball, memory power, business, New Jersey history, and travel. The lives of American figures of distinction are a particular area of interest for him. He has written numerous books for Mitchell Lane Publishers, including *Pedro Menendez de Aviles, Philo Farnsworth Invents TV, Robert Goddard, Bernardo de Galvez,* and *Where Did the Dinosaurs Go?* He lives in Bordentown, New Jersey, with his family and a fat, fuzzy, and crafty calico cat named Rusti.

PHOTO CREDITS: Cover—Getty Images; pp. 1, 3—Texas State Library & Archives Commission; p. 4—Barbara Marvis; pp. 7, 8—Getty Images; p. 9—Library of Congress; pp. 10, 12—Northwind Picture Archives; p. 14—Library of Congress; p. 15—Northwind Picture Archives; pp. 16, 18, 20—Corbis; p. 22—Northwind Picture Archives; pp. 24, 26—Corbis

TABLE OF CONTENTS

Words in **bold** type can be found in the glossary.

The Alamo as it appears in modern times, in San Antonio, Texas. The site has been operated as a shrine by the Daughters of the Republic of Texas since 1905. More than two million people visit the Alamo each year.

The Alamo

On a cold quiet morning on the Texas plains in early March, 1836, one hundred eighty-nine Texas freedom fighters were sleeping inside the Alamo. Some were lying down. Some were sitting against the walls. They all had their guns ready.

Outside it was still dark. The late winter sun was not yet up. The air was calm and chilly. Frost hugged the ground. Inside the Alamo, all was quiet. Outside were several thousand Mexican soldiers.

The Alamo was not supposed to be a fort. It was built as a **mission**. Its four walls were not sturdy. It was hard to defend, but it was all this group of **Texians** (TEK-see-ins) had.

In 1836, Texas was a part of Mexico. Mexico wanted to keep Texas. The Texians wanted Texas to be free and independent. For thirteen days, the small group of Texians had held off the much larger Mexican army. How much longer could they do so?

During the day, the Mexican soldiers would shoot cannonballs at the Alamo walls. At night the Texians tried to fix the damage. They did not sleep much. They tried to sleep during the day, but the roar of the cannons kept them awake. This went on for several days. By the night of March 5, the Texians were very tired.

That night the Texians fell into a deep sleep. They did not see the Mexican soldiers getting ready to attack. The Mexicans circled the Alamo. They lay on the ground. The darkness hid them. They waited. Nobody made a sound.

Inside the Alamo was a man named Davy Crockett. He was a famous hunter. He had also been in Congress. Now he was fighting for Texas.

Suddenly a Mexican soldier shouted. Then others did too. They jumped up. They

Davy Crockett called this image "the only correct likeness that has been taken of me." It is based on a portrait of him painted late in 1833.

This painting reveals the way many people think Davy Crockett fought at the Alamo—swinging his gun like a club at the enemy soldiers. But this is just one version of the battle, and it may not be correct.

An engraving shows how the Alamo looked around 1844, just eight years after the battle. Compare this with the picture on page 4 of how the Alamo looks in modern times, and notice the differences.

ran toward the Alamo. The Texians jumped up too. Gunfire shattered the early morning quiet.

Davy Crockett and the Texians fought hard, but there were too many enemy soldiers. The Mexicans swarmed into the Alamo.

Crockett looked around. There were Mexican soldiers everywhere! He had been in tight spots before. Always he had gotten out of them. Could he get out of this one too?

Davy Crockett was a very good hunter. Hunting relaxed him, and it provided food for his family. In a book he wrote about his life, he claimed he killed 105 bears in one year.

Young Davy

David Crockett was born on August 17, 1786, in Greene County in eastern Tennessee. His parents were John and Rebecca Hawkins Crockett.

Davy's family moved a lot. His father tried different ways to make money. He was a farmer and a **tavern** owner. He ran a **gristmill**. Nothing seemed to work. He never had much money.

When Davy was twelve, he left home for the first time. He helped a man take care of cows. He also did many other jobs, such as helping a **wagoner**. He would bring the money he earned back to his family. This started a pattern in Davy's life. He never stayed in one place too long.

In 1806 Davy married a girl named Polly Finley. They had two boys, John Wesley and

Homes on the frontier looked much different from modern houses. Most homes were built using whatever material was available, since there were no stores at which to buy supplies. Crockett might have lived in a log house similar to this one.

William. They also had a girl named Margaret. Davy hunted for food. He enjoyed hunting and was good at it. Like his father, he found it hard to make money.

In 1813, Crockett joined the war against the Creek Indians. Polly begged him not to go. She was scared to be alone with the children. Davy went anyway. When he returned home in 1815, Polly was sick. Soon she died. Davy then married a **widow** named Elizabeth Patton, but he always missed Polly.

Crockett kept moving his family. Finally they settled in western Tennessee. At this time there were only twenty-four states in America. Western Tennessee was not developed. There were no stores and few roads. There was just the woods filled with animals. People had to either hunt or farm for food.

Crockett hunted with a rifle he called Betsey. He was an excellent **marksman**. His hunting trips sometimes took months. They often kept him away from home. Elizabeth had to raise his children and take care of their

Hunters on the frontier had to take whatever opportunities they could to shoot wild game, because their families depended on them to find food.

home without him. It was lonely and hard for her. She did not like that Davy was always away. They argued about it.

In 1817, Crockett became a **justice of the peace**. It was his first public office. Then in 1821 he was elected to the Tennessee **legislature**.

People said that Crockett should run for Congress. At first he laughed. Then he thought about it. Could someone from the Tennessee woods go to Congress? He decided to find out.

A covered wagon crosses the Cumberland River in Kentucky in the
early 1800s. Without an organized system of roads, bridges, and
tunnels, traveling was difficult and dangerous. Even so, Crockett often
moved with his family.

Crockett campaigns for Congress from atop a stump. He was very good at meeting the voters in small groups. He would talk, joke, tell stories, and answer their questions.

Congressman Crockett

Crockett ran for Congress in 1825. People liked him. But they also liked his opponent, Adam Alexander. Crockett lost by just 267 votes.

He felt bad about losing, so he decided to find a way to make money. He loaded barrel **staves** onto some small boats. He wanted to bring the staves to a city and sell them. The boats hit a sunken tree in the river. They broke apart. The staves were swept downstream, and Crockett almost drowned!

In 1827, Crockett ran for Congress again. Many more people had moved to the woods. When Crockett spoke, he told jokes and stories. Once a group of guinea fowl started chattering next to where his opponent was giving a speech. Davy joked that the birds were yelling, "Crockett, Crockett, Crockett." He laughed, and everyone else did too.

Crockett arrives to see a large gathering in Louisville, Kentucky. As he became famous, more and more people wanted to see him and hear him speak.

At first his opponents did not take him seriously. They thought he was just a hunter. Too late they realized that he was a serious candidate.

People trusted Davy. He was like them. He talked to them in language they could understand. He said he would be their friend in Congress. He won the election.

At first Crockett worried about Congress. He thought he would not fit in. He was from the woods. Most members of Congress were not. He wore hunting clothes. Most members of Congress wore fancy suits. Would they laugh at him?

Some people did laugh. Crockett ignored them and got to work. He tried to pass a **bill** that let people buy land cheaply. Congress did not pass the bill. Instead the members made speeches about other things. This annoyed him.

"There's too much talk," Crockett said about Congress. But the speeches continued.

Davy Crockett wearing his typical hunting clothes. This picture was painted in 1889 by William Henry Huddle.

Famous Davy

Crockett kept trying to get his land bill passed. It never happened. He was reelected to Congress in 1829 and tried again. Again he had no luck.

Other people noticed Crockett. They liked the way he spoke. They liked how he acted. They talked about him. The newspapers wrote about him. Soon everyone was reading and talking about Davy Crockett.

In 1831, a man wrote a play called *The Lion of the West*. The main character was named Nimrod Wildfire, but everyone knew it was really Davy Crockett. The play was very popular. The author made money.

Some politicians were jealous of Crockett. They worried about the attention he got. They thought he might become too powerful. They did not want that. They helped defeat Crockett in the next election.

Crockett did not stay defeated for long. In 1833 he ran for Congress again and won. Back in Congress, it was the same old story. He could not get his land bill passed.

A common flintlock musket. Crockett used one of these muskets at the Alamo. No one knows what happened to Crocket's gun after the battle. It was either thrown away or taken by someone as a souvenir.

Crockett was still famous. A man wrote a book about him. People bought every single copy. The author made money. Crockett did not make money from either the play or book.

The book told **tall tales** about him. It said he would brag and boast. It said he was "half-horse and half-alligator." That was supposed to make him seem tough. Instead it made him look silly. Crockett did not brag and boast. He did not even like to be called Davy. He preferred David.

Crockett decided to write his own book that would tell people the truth about him. He also hoped it would make him some money.

The book was popular. In it, he wrote: "Be always sure you're right—*then go ahead.*" The book made him even more famous. He got a new hunting rifle as a gift. He named it Pretty Betsey.

Politicians grew more jealous of Crockett. They worried that he might run for president of the United States. That scared them. In 1835 they again helped defeat him for reelection.

Crockett decided to go on an adventure to forget the loss. He went to Texas.

This nineteenth-century illustration shows Crockett at the Alamo, again fighting many enemy soldiers. It strengthens the tall tale that Crockett killed hundreds of enemy soldiers that day. In truth, once the Mexican army got inside the walls of the Alamo compound, there were too many of them for the defenders to fight.

How Did Crockett Die?

Crockett joined the Texians in the Alamo. He played his fiddle to entertain them. The Texians were happy he was there. They were probably also glad because he was such a good shot.

When the Mexican soldiers attacked in the early morning of March 6, 1836, the Texians could not stop them. All the Texians defending the Alamo were killed, including Davy Crockett. No one knows how Crockett died, but there are many theories.

Some people say that Crockett died fighting. They say that he killed many enemy soldiers before he fell.

Others think that he tried to escape over the Alamo wall with other Texians. Mexican

Statues of Davy Crockett, like this one in Ozona, Texas, are scattered throughout the United States. Davy is one of the most popular figures in the history of the United States. He continues to live in story and song as an American hero.

soldiers were waiting outside. They killed the Texians who tried to escape.

Still others think that Crockett was captured and then killed. They think this because a Mexican soldier wrote it in his diary. But are the stories in the diary real? No one knows.

No one knows how Crockett died. Probably, no one will ever know.

Today Crockett is still famous. Most people know something about him. He is written about in songs and stories. There are movies and television shows about him. Some of them are accurate. Some are filled with tall tales.

Crockett was a brave man. He faced the dangers of the wilderness. He stood up for people's rights. Many people liked and respected him.

Davy Crockett died fighting for freedom. He died trying to help others. Solving the mystery of his death is not as important as knowing how he lived.

CHRONOLOGY

1786 Born on August 17 in Greene County, Tennessee

1798 Leaves home for first time

1806 Marries Mary "Polly" Finley

1807 Son John Wesley is born

1809 Son William is born

1812 Daughter Margaret is born

1813 Fights in Creek Indian War

1815 Polly Crockett dies; Davy marries Elizabeth Patton

1817 Becomes a justice of the peace

1821 Is elected to Tennessee State Legislature

1823 Is reelected to Tennessee State Legislature

1825 Is defeated in first try for Congress

1826 Almost drowns on Mississippi River

1827 Is elected to Congress

1829 Is reelected to Congress

1831 Is defeated for Congress

1833 Is reelected to Congress

1834 Publishes *Davy Crockett: His Own Story; A Narrative of the Life of David Crockett of the State of Tennessee*

1835 Is defeated for Congress; goes to Texas

1836 Dies at the Alamo on March 6

TIMELINE IN HISTORY

1775   Daniel Boone begins blazing the Wilderness Road.

1776   Declaration of Independence is signed.

1777   Vermont becomes a colony and abolishes slavery there.

1781   The British surrender at Yorktown effectively ends the American Revolution.

1793   First balloon flight in the United States goes from Philadelphia, Pennsylvania, to Deptford, New Jersey.

1804   Alexander Hamilton is fatally wounded by Aaron Burr in a duel.

1806   Zebulon Pike begins exploring southwestern United States.

1811   New Madrid, Missouri, is hit by one of the greatest earthquakes in American history.

1812   War of 1812 begins.

1816   New England receives ten inches of snow in June in the "year without a summer."

1825   American colonization of Texas is authorized.

1833   First streetcar is put into operation in New York City.

1836   Texas freedom fighters battle Mexican soldiers at the Alamo.

1840   First dental school in the world is founded in Baltimore.

1846   Alexander Cartwright organizes first set of modern baseball rules.

1859   First hotel passenger elevator is installed in a New York hotel.

1869   The transcontinental railroad is completed.

FIND OUT MORE

Books

Harmon, Daniel E. *Davy Crockett.* Philadelphia: Chelsea House Publishers, 2002.

Parks, Aileen Wells. *Davy Crockett: Young Rifleman.* Childhood of Famous Americans. Reprint. New York: Simon and Schuster, 1986.

Sanford, William R., and Carl R. Green. *Davy Crockett: Defender of the Alamo.* Springfield, New Jersey: Enslow Publishers, 1996.

Works Consulted

Blair, Walter. *Davy Crockett, Legendary Frontier Hero: His True Life Story and the Fabulous Tall Tales Told about Him.* Springfield, Illinois: Lincoln-Herndon Press, 1986.

Crockett, David. *A Narrative of the Life of David Crockett.* Reprint. Lincoln: University of Nebraska Press, 1987.

Derr, Mark. *The Frontiersman – The Real Life and Many Legends of Davy Crockett.* New York: William Morrow and Company, Inc. 1993.

Townsend, Tom. *Davy Crockett: An American Hero.* Austin, Texas: Eakin Press, 1987.

On the Internet

The Alamo–San Antonio, TX
  http://www.thealamo.org/

American West–"Davy Crockett"
  http://www.americanwest.com/pages/davycroc.htm

David (Davy) Crockett Memorial Home Page
  http://www.pointsouth.com/csanet/greatmen/crockett/crockett.htm

The Official Davy Crockett Family Homepage
  http://www.goahead.org

GLOSSARY

bill (BILL)—A proposed law.

gristmill (GRIST-mill)—A mill for grinding grain.

justice of the peace (JUS-tis uv thuh PEES)—A local public official who can hear minor criminal and civil cases and pass judgment, and perform other functions.

legislature (LED-jis-lay-chur)—A group of elected officials who make laws.

marksman (MARKS-man)—A person who can shoot a gun on target.

mission (MIH-shun)—A church.

stave (STAYV)—One of the thin, narrow pieces of wood that form the sides of a barrel or cask.

tall tales (TALL TAYLS)—A type of frontier story that overstates the truth in an entertaining or funny way.

tavern (TAA-vern)—An inn; also, a gathering place where alcoholic drinks are served.

Texian (TEK-see-in)—A person who lived in Texas before it became a state.

wagoner (WAA-guh-ner)—A person who drives a wagon.

widow (WIH-doh)—A woman whose husband has died.

INDEX